Stan,

Thank you for
all your support!
Let's get our prosperity Now!

FINANCIAL
Fornication

Avoid Financial & Credit Dis-Ease

TARRA JACKSON

ISBN: 0-615-50162-1

ISBN-13: 978-061-550162-8

DEDICATION

For my beloved son, Roger-D,

Learn from mommy's mistakes.

I love you!

For my baby sister, Tia Jackson-Truitt, MSW, LCSW,

Thank you for saying, "Girl, you need to write a book!"

The first copy is yours!

I love you!

For my baby brothers & sisters: Tonilia Stanford,

Stephani Jackson, Aaron Stanford, and Jerome Stanford,

I'm watching you! So don't mess up…like your big sis did

when she was your age.

I love you!

"As a military member, I believe that Financial Fornication is a must read for all in the military. One of the benefits of the military is that it returns young men and women back to society a better person, by strengthen their mental and physical well-being. This book adds a third dynamic element to this strengthening equation of Financial Fortitude. This is one of the best pieces of financial armor a military member can buy."

Gunnery Sergeant Madyun M. Shahid
United States Marine Corp

"Upon reading this book, I began to see clearly the plan of God for every believer & how the enemy would love to stop their financial blessing from moving forward. This book will reveal how to pay more attention to their financial lifestyle and become more aware of the enemy's tactics using financial temptations. Be blessed as you read this powerful and anointed book."

Pastor Rod C. Tate
Assistant to the Senior Pastor
The Greater Piney Grove Baptist Church

FOREWORD

Have you realized it's easier for many to discuss sex rather than money? Is this because the topic of sex is discussed openly in our culture on a regular basis? We see it on television and hear it in popular songs so much that it has become commonplace and our senses has become numb. Many parents take a lot of time to make sure their children understand the pitfalls of being sexually promiscuous, but neglect to prepare their children for the fiscal realities that that can have devastating effects on our lives. When I really began to think about why this was so, it hit me! Sex is easier to discuss because we've been led to believe that it's easier to have and manage than money.

When Tarra first informed me that she was writing a book, I was thrilled to hear it. But I must admit that I was a little thrown by the risqué title "Financial Fornication". But I quickly became clear on the concept as I realized we can't help to be intrigued when we see the words fornication following finances. I immediately thought, what a great way to get individuals attention by any means necessary, using the correlation of money and sexual relationships (two very vital subjects) as the concept to deliver a message that will promote change and empowerment.

I had been aware of Tarra's passion to educate individuals on the importance of being financially literate and applauded her efforts. She possesses a wealth of knowledge and has a voice that needs to be heard to empower individuals to build strong financial lives, and to her credit has found a method that gets their attention.

Serving as a personal finance coach, I speak to many groups and organizations around the country about the importance of fiscal responsibility, but have realized when you say financial literacy many people check out mentally. To the contrary if you mention sex and relationships to the same crowd they become intrigued and want to hear more. Mostly because it's more exciting to talk about something that gives us pleasure. But can't being fiscally responsible serve as the gift that keeps on giving exponentially?

We have become disconnected from our fiscal lives, thus avoiding money talks at all cost unless we are talking about our dreams and wants of obtaining it. We often shy away from exploring our current economic situation to avoid facing reality, in exchange for what we'd like it to be or have. Sure, there is nothing wrong with dreaming, but in order to make the dream of financial security a reality we must have an understanding of our current financial picture, know how we got there and be willing to use the error of our ways as lessons or stepping stones to get us to where we really want or need to be. Instead we become stuck, live our lives by default and fall victim to poor savings and spending habits.

FINANCIAL FORNICATION

Financial Fornication is a unique approach to a topic that many of us would benefit from hearing in order to protect our financial interest. By using sexual undertones to speak about a taboo subject such as personal finances, Tarra gets the reader's attention and uses this concept to serve as a creative way to engage individuals to think before they embark on a journey that may lead to financial ruin. Many of us learn about finances through default and make expensive mistakes that cost us more than we could ever imagine.

Instant gratification has taken the place of saving and making smart purchase decisions. We have a clouded view of our needs versus wants, thus result to living in the moment and not thinking about the consequences. Financial fornication makes it plain and delivers a timely message in an apropos method that effectively paints a vivid picture of the things we need to master our financial situation.

Many of us feel that we spend therefore we are. This is a concept that Financial Fornication alters by alerting us that our purchases don't make us. We often believe that buying makes us feel better, important, justified and even complete, but these feelings pass as our purchases become old and our debt grows into a burden.

Our desire to have because we feel we lack results in urges that become difficult to control and later debt that begins to mount leaving us feeling hopeless. Financial Fornication is the antidote to treating what ails us financially. Filled with tips and tools to help you see the error of your ways and understand that ignorance is truly not bliss. Tarra Jackson takes us on a ride that will assist in painting a visual that becomes embedded in our psyche.

Written by someone who has experienced setbacks, but has been able to bounce back, Tarra realizes what is needed to make this important transition to obtain control of our financial lives. By simply stating the facts and showing us the errors of our ways, this book serves as the catalyst to get us thinking, educated and on the right track to financial freedom. This lesson in literacy serves as the equivalent of being sat down and taught about the birds and the bees, but instead of sex education it's a financial education that will allow you the freedom to realize the importance of avoiding substantial revolving debt, understanding credit and making sound financial decisions that will change your life for the better and help our financial dreams become reality.

Clyde Anderson
Financial Lifestyle Coach
CNN Financial Contributor
Author of "Time Out! 21 Day's to Discipline: How to Control Your Thought To Achieve Financial Success"

CONTENTS

FOREWORD i

ACKNOWLEDGMENTS vii

INTRODUCTION xi

1 WHAT IS FINANCIAL FORNICATION? 1

2 FINANCIAL ONE NIGHT STANDS 7

3 ARE YOU FINANCIALLY PROMISCUOUS? 11

4 DO YOU HAVE FINANCIAL STDs? 15

5 WHAT IS FINANCIAL DATING? 27

6 THE 80% RULE 35

7 ARE YOU BEING FINANCIALLY ABUSED? 39

8 FINANCIAL ABSTINENCE 51

9 THE CREDIT GAME: BOOK SNEAK PREVIEW 55

10 THE CONCLUSION: THE TALK 63

APPENDIX: BLANK WORKSHEETS 69

AM I FINANCIALLY PROMISCUOUS? 71

DO I HAVE FINANCIAL STDS? 72

BUILDING MY BUDGET / SPENDING PLAN 73

MY FINANCIAL DEAL MAKERS & DEAL BREAKERS 74

HOW DEEP IS MY FINANCIAL RELATIONSHIP? 75

RESOURCES 77

ABOUT THE AUTHOR 79

ACKNOWLEDGMENTS

There are so many people who have been instrumental in my personal and professional development and deserve recognition. Unfortunately, to list everyone's name individually would be longer than this book itself. For everyone who I have met one time or thousands of times, who has been in my life for a minute or a season or a lifetime, who I have listened to or have shared information with, who has been my teacher or my student, whom I've experience like, love, hate or all three; you all have shaped me and continue to make me into the woman and professional God has for me to be.

I humbly and formally give thanks to God for loving me because of and in spite of and especially for His favor!

My son, Roger-D, for always taking care of his mommy, no matter what! You are my heart and my "road dog!" Love you.

My immediate family: Daddy and Mom (Bobby & Stephanie Jackson), Rev. Mommom Jean Wilson (aka Momi), Poppop "Big Ruff" Roger Wilson (aka Popi), my favorite Uncle Darrell "Buster Brown" Wilson, my baby sis Titi (Tia Jackson-Truitt), and Barr (Jabarr Truitt), you have always been there for me. I would not be successful without your support. I love you. My extended family: the Jacksons

(Opelika, AL), Wilsons (Laurel, DE), Allens & Maulls (Pinetown/Lewes, DE), Stanfords (California, Delaware, & Maryland), and Aunt Betty Washington (my favorite Mani / Pedi partner), and all of my extended family; I thank God for allowing me to be a part of you.

My BFFs; my surrogate little sister, Velecia McNeel (yes, I am the boss of you because I am older) and my twin, Gerald Robinson (I get you because you get me), for always being there for me when I needed you and for checking me when you knew I needed it.

The African-American Credit Union Coalition for allowing me to learn, to share, and to grow amongst such phenomenal credit union CEOs, Executives and Volunteers. You are my mentors. Thank you for showing me why and how credit unions are a Movement not an industry.

Special thanks and acknowledgement to the Board of Directors, colleagues, staff, and membership of Credit Union of Atlanta, "where we work for our *members' financial well-being* every day" and for the significant investments and contributions made in the community and the Movement! Thank you Ms. Sheilah Montgomery, CUA President/CEO, for being such a great mentor and for helping me realize that "It really isn't that deep!" ☺ Thank you for sharing.

Thank you Calvary Baptist Church in Dover, Delaware, Pastor Rev. Dr. & Mrs. Richard M. Avant and Assistant Pastor (Uncle) Norman & Minister (Aunt) Cynthia Fields and the entire congregation for being such a powerfully spiritual part of my life.

Min. Paul Q. Fortson (aka Pastor), thank you for seeing my vision and for your encouragement ... "Stretch out your rod, Shawty!" Thank you, Bishop Paul Fortson, for being such a powerful man of God. Mark (Kev) Fortson, you get a shout out for always making me laugh! I have fallen in love with Paradise Church of God in Christ, Atlanta, GA. Thank you for being my spiritual home away from home.

Shout out to Crunk For Christ Radio for all of your support! (www.crunkforchristradio.com). Who knew that there was Hip Hop Christian Music? I love it!

My personal and professional coaches: Dr. Michelle Brown, Catalyst Enterprises, Inc.; Ms. Renee Sattiewhite, Sattiewhite Training Production and Muriel Garr. Long walks, late night phone calls to finishing projects, mood swings, tears, and you still managed to love me and coach me through it all. Wow!

Clyde Anderson, author and CNN Financial Contributor, God placed you in my life for a reason. I think I know why. I'll Facebook you later. (Smile) Can't wait to read your next book!

John Hope Bryant, founder and President of Operation Hope, you are a revolutionary and visionary leader of Financial Literacy. I want to be like you when I grow up! Thank you for all that you do in the Financial Education Movement for our youth and communities through the Banking On Our Future program.

Thank you to all of my Facebook Friends for your participation in building my first book. Your feedback, suggestions, and encouragement helped me through this interesting process.

Thank you to my editor, Mary Wright (one of the best wordsmiths in Atlanta, GA) and my content editor, LaKesha Crawford (next round of raw oysters are on me!).

Thank you to my graphic designer, William Lee or Lee Graphix (www.LeeGraphix.com). You are so talented!

Thank you for sharing your talents and encouragement during this journey.

Spark Plug, publisher of People You Need To Know magazine, thank you for seeing in me what I didn't know was there. Thank you for your advice and guidance. You are truly a marketing maverick!

Last but not least, thank you to the love of my life for getting me, supporting me, and for your (sometimes brutal) honesty no matter what. You were there for me during one of the most challenging times of my professional career. You kept me focused and calm through it all. I've thanked you numerous times, but I again have to say, Thank you for being my friend!

For those that I did not specifically name, charge it to the head, the limited space, or the confidentiality agreement (smile) and not the heart! Thank you to … (you know who you are). I appreciate you all so much!

INTRODUCTION

Before I get on my high horse about my interpretation of financial relationships, I must disclose the following and appropriate disclaimers. So, here goes...

Disclaimer #1: The opinions and statements made in this book are my own and in no way represent any organization that I may be employed with now or in the future... (Unless...you know).

Disclaimer #2: This book does not encourage the mental, physical or spiritual act of fornication. The word, its meaning, and other related terms are only used to show the parallels of potentially negative consequences of these acts in a financial manner.

Disclaimer #3: I am a financial professional and will continue to learn as the economy and technologies change. Therefore, I do not consider myself to be an expert. (I really don't consider most "experts" to be experts, but I digress.) Based on my education (shout out to Delaware State University & Strayer University), my professional experience in the financial services industry (Love my Credit Unions), and my good and bad personal experiences and relationship with finances and credit, I consider myself to be a Professional Opinionist!

Disclaimer #4: I relate and connect to my clients because I have personally and professionally dealt with credit adversities.

Now that I got that out of the way, here goes...

It seems that people are more inclined to talk about sex than any other subject, especially credit and finances. So, let's talk about both.

I've observed that people deal with financial / credit relationships similar to how they deal with their personal relationships. Whether healthy or dysfunctional, financial and personal relationships are a significant part of a person's being. If dysfunctional, it is imperative to identify the source of the dysfunction, change the destructive behavior, remove yourself from an abusive situation, and execute positive and helpful behaviors or medication, if necessary.

Many people are suffering in silence in Financially Abusive relationships and are apprehensive to leave a financial institution because they think and feel that they owe the financial institution too much and with their "colorful credit," no other financial institution will want them. In this book we will not only discuss how to get out of a Financially Abusive relationship with a financial institution, we will define Financial Fornication, discuss how to identify if we are being Financially Promiscuous, determine if we may have acquired Financial STDs, discover if we are having long-term relationships with Financial One Night Stands, when to be Financially Abstinent and ways to cure Financial Dis-Eases. We will also talk about why it is important and how to Financially Date.

Since financial literacy is not mandatory or a required class in schools, many people learn from their parents (but wait ...who did they learn from???), or by default after they get their first credit card after high school or their first car loan. They end up learning the hard way when they get introduced to the collections department if/when they stop or don't pay as agreed. They realize the impact of this action when they mature and try to buy their first home or get their dream job. The unfortunate part of this is that they do not learn how to have a productive and positive relationship with credit. Credit is meant to be leverage not a hindrance! And "please understand" ... *Ignorance is not bliss, it's Expensive*! The less you know, the more you'll pay, and the more financial institutions will make.

Financial Fornication is a book to help us begin the process of establishing and growing a healthy and beneficial Financial Relationship. This book provides the opportunity for you to participate. Therefore, this can be the beginning of a helpful dialog.

I look forward to beginning this process with you and becoming a resource to you in the future.

Yours in the journey,
Tarra R. Jackson
June 2011

1 WHAT IS FINANCIAL FORNICATION?

A male friend of mine "accidentally" went into a conference for single women to discuss why they were single. It had a panel of men to answer the single women's questions about relationships and why men choose to or not to get married. When he realized where he was, he decided to hang around to hear the types of questions the women would ask and what the men's responses would be.

He told me about one woman who stood at the microphone and asked the panel of "single" men, "When is a good time to sleep with a man?" Bless her heart, I thought. He continued to share that the men on the panel gave their answers like, "After three months." or "When he does this or that..." Typical, I thought again. The last man to respond, he explained, took a deep breath and answered matter-of-factly, "The only time you should sleep with a man is when you're married to him." Wow!!! What a profound statement from a man, I thought, yet again.

A few weeks later after I had been interviewed on a radio show at a university in Atlanta one evening, several students that were working in the studio decided to ask me financial questions. One of the students inquired, "Ms. Jackson, I just got a new credit card in the mail and I want to buy some clothes, a laptop, this flat screen TV, etc. Should I purchase them with the credit card?"

I asked the student, "Do you have a job?"

He responded, "Work study at the university to help pay my tuition."

"Do you have savings?" I inquired.

"Not really! But my parents send me money from time to time or when I need it."

Awww Lawd, I thought. I took a deep breath and answered matter-of-factly, "Well, the only time you should purchase items like that is when you have the money saved up to buy them."

The conversation with the college student helped me to realize that his anxiousness, curiosity, and desires of using credit to buy things he wanted was similar to those same feelings that people have when it comes to personal and physical relationships. The microwave mentality, of wanting what we want when we want it ... NOW, is becoming more and more prevalent in today's society. Instant gratification is taking over the value of waiting for the right mate or waiting until we have saved up enough money to make certain purchases.

Today, in most cases instead of saving up for that new laptop, a consumer may use their credit card to purchase it. Then when the bill comes in, they may only make the minimum payment. Then there is that flat screen TV that they put on their credit card and again only make the minimum payment or don't pay it off.

Financial Fornication is the excessive and compulsive use of revolving credit or other unsecured credit (not secured by collateral) for items or purchases that are not significant or could be paid with cash.

2

We sometimes try to justify the act of Financial Fornication by telling ourselves, "I don't want to use up all of my savings (the little I have)." "If I don't get it now, I might miss the sale and then I'll have to pay more, later." "I deserve to be happy, so I'm going to live for today and get what I want!"

So, we use that credit card to purchase that cruise to the Bahamas, instead of saving up for it or using the cash payment plan available. Now, what was supposed to be a **Financial One Night Stand** turns into a **Financial Long-Term Relationship** that may become **Financially Abusive** and if we are being **Financially Promiscuous**, we run the risk of catching **Financial STDs**. We'll review these matters in the next few chapters.

For now, let's get a few statistics out of the way…

- **"Total U.S. revolving debt (98 percent of which is made up of credit card debt): $852.6 billion, as of March 2010."** (Source: "Federal Reserve's G.19 report on consumer credit," March 2010)

  Reality Check: The U.S. has a severe case of Financial STDs.

- **"Only 2 percent of undergraduates had no credit history."** (Source: Sallie Mae, "How Undergraduate Students Use Credit Cards," April 2009)

  We will call them Financial Virgins.

- **"Undergraduates are carrying record-high credit card balances. The average balance grew to $3,173, the highest in the years the study has been conducted. Median debt grew from 2004's $946 to $1,645. Twenty-one percent of undergraduates had balances of between $3,000 and $7,000, also up from the last study."** (Source: Sallie Mae, "How Undergraduate Students Use Credit Cards," April 2009)

  Reality Check: Consumers are being Financially Promiscuous at an early age.

- **Average unsecured debt per household with credit card debt: $15,788***
  * Calculated by dividing the total revolving debt in the U.S. ($852.6 billion as of March 2010 data, as listed in the Federal Reserve's May 2010 report on consumer credit) by the estimated number of households carrying credit card debt (54 million)

  Reality Check: Financial & Credit Dis-Ease affects and infects the entire family/household.

A wonderful friend of mine told me one day, "We spend the Most when we feel the Least!" WOW!!! *"Studies also show that people with low self-esteem engage in more impulse spending and buy things they don't need." Deborah Fowless, about.com.* Therefore, spending money is psychological.

Everyone has a "vice" and most vices cost money in some way. I tell people all of the time that my vice is FOOD! When I feel the least, I EAT! And my favorite chef is McDonald's. It's just something about that special sauce on the Big Mac that makes the world seem like a better place when everything is going wrong. I will also frequent my favorite Bistro in Atlanta to get my favorite meal more often. That costs money!!!

Other people's vices may be shopping. Ok, I have fallen in love with buying suits and shoes... and you can't forget the matching purse. It's just something about that transaction that gets my endorphins going, increases the serotonin to my brain and makes the day so much brighter.

It's called the **Pleasure Principle**. *"The pleasure principle is the driving force of the ID that seeks immediate gratification of all needs, wants, and urges. In other words, the pleasure principle strives to fulfill our most basic and primitive urges, including hunger, thirst, anger, and sex. When these needs are not met, the result is a state of anxiety or tension." - Sigmund Freud.*

I have concluded that spending money fits into this definition as well. Our need to have because we feel we lack may cause us to have the same basic and primitive urge to buy whatever it is we feel or think we need or want.

The problem may not lie with the actual purchases; it is usually with how we ultimately handle the credit balance when the monthly credit card bill arrives. If the balance is paid off in full, when the statement arrives, FABULOUS!!! But, if the balance is not paid off, and more purchases are made using the credit card or line of credit, and the new credit balance is not paid in full, a long-term financial relationship has been established with multiple Financial One Night Stands.

2 FINANCIAL ONE NIGHT STANDS

What is a Financial One-Night Stand? Glad you asked!

A Financial One-Night Stand is supposed to be a One Time Financial Transaction. It's paid with cash or in full when the credit card bill is received.

Many people take those Financial One-Night Stands, like purchasing a big screen TV or a couple of pairs of designer shoes, and charge it to their credit card with 18% to 30% interest. Now that $2,000 (for the TV) at 18% interest, with a minimum payment of 3% ($60.00) will take 47 months (that's 4 years and 3 months or 1,551 days) to pay it off. Will you still have that TV in four years? That Financial One Night Stand may turn into an undesired and expensive Long Term Financial Relationship.

Let's check out Jackie Consumer's story. Jackie Consumer is just like most middle class consumers. She has a job and makes decent money. One day Jackie was out at the mall with her best friend and sister. As they browsed through a few stores, Jackie thought to herself, "These sales are the best!" Then she saw it … THAT! To Jackie "THAT" was about 3 or 4 cute Corporate Sexy suits. In those perfectly angled lights and through her "One Day Sale Only" blurry vision, the sales prices for those suits looked pretty good...real good! They fit her perfectly! The sales person grabbed her attention and told her everything she wanted to hear, including how great she looked in all of the suits... but she knew that! She was mentally aroused. So she decided to not only buy one of the suits but to buy all four of them! While at the register the salesperson asked Jackie, "Will this be cash or credit?" Without thinking too deep, she busted out her new platinum credit card (yes...Platinum!!!) and executed what is supposed to be a One Time Transaction.

About 30 days later Jackie got her platinum credit card statement. It only required her to make a minimum payment of $25.00. Jackie decided that based on her "budget" that month she would be able to pay $50.00 towards the balance. This was the beginning of Jackie's Financial Long-Term Relationship with what should have been a Financial One-Night Stand. About six months later her balance quadrupled because she was a bit financially promiscuous and had numerous financial one-night stands with that platinum credit card. Jackie wanted to break up with her credit card company because it turned into a financially abusive relationship with their ridiculously high interest rate. But she felt trapped because she was late with payments a few times and the credit card company had to blab it out to everyone on her credit reports. Now all of the new creditors that she was trying to get into a new financial relationship with knew how financially promiscuous she was along with her payment flaws.

Jackie found a financial institution that she wanted to have a financial long-term relationship with, because she wanted to finance her first home, but they didn't want her. They declined her application because of her financial reputation. Jackie's financial promiscuity and inconsistent payment history turned what was supposed to be a Financial One Night Stand into a Financial Nightmare and burden. Ouch!

Are you being financially promiscuous? Let's find out.

3 ARE YOU FINANCIALLY PROMISCUOUS?

When a consumer indiscriminately executes financial transactions on a casual basis using unsecured or revolving credit haphazardly with multiple financial institutions, this is considered Financial Promiscuity.

Being financially promiscuous will make a consumer vulnerable to Financial STDs. Not only will Financial STDs negatively impact a consumer's finances, overall credit management and credit score, it may affect and infect their physical health and family relationships due to the stress it may produce.

As previously noted, using revolving credit, like credit cards haphazardly to purchase "things" is relatively psychological. Sometimes a consumer may purchase things like food, alcohol, electronics, clothing, gifts for others, etc., when it may really not necessary or affordable, just to help themselves "feel" better. When they do this, they run the risk of being Financially Promiscuous. And if they don't think about the consequences and protect themselves by using a Financial "Contraceptive," also known as a Budget or Spending Plan, then they will acquire a Financial Dis-Ease, or worse, Financial STDs.

Before we talk about Financial STDs let's first identify if you may be financially promiscuous.

❑ YES   ❑ NO   Are you using more and more of your income to pay towards your debt?

❑ YES   ❑ NO   Are you only making the minimum payments on your revolving credit cards or lines of credit?

❑ YES   ❑ NO   Are you using your credit card to pay bills or things that should be paid with cash?

❑ YES   ❑ NO   Are you paying bills with money that should be used to pay another bill or that should be saved to pay something else of importance? ("Robbing Peter to pay Paul?")

❑ YES   ❑ NO   If your credit card is declined when used, do you pull out another credit card (praying that the transaction will go through) because you did not have enough cash or money in your bank account to cover the purchase?

❑ YES   ❑ NO   Are you frequently or sometimes late with your payments on credit obligations?

❑ YES   ❑ NO   Have you maxed out your credit cards or are you near the credit limit(s)?

❑ YES   ❑ NO   If you were approved for a loan or credit card at one financial institution, would you or have you gone to another financial institution to apply for more credit?

SOMETHING TO THINK ABOUT: If you answered YES to any one of the questions, you may be considered Financial Promiscuous and susceptible to Financial STDs.

4 DO YOU HAVE FINANCIAL STDs?

Financial STD stands for Substantially Tremendous Debt. This is a common financial disease of Financial Promiscuity. Too much debt, especially revolving and unsecured (not secured by collateral), with too many financial institutions will cause this unwanted and unfavorable financial condition.

Financial Dis-Ease can be described as a financial disorder resulting in inadequate finances triggered by the effects of unemployment, furlough (reduction in work hours), sudden medical or family emergency expense, unanticipated or unforeseen expenses, poor money management, excessive spending (financial promiscuity), or the lack of financial education.

Some **common symptoms** of Financial STDs are:
1. Growing debt
2. Increasing required minimum payments for debt
3. Using cash advances from credit cards to pay other credit or monthly household bills
4. Inconsistent, missed, or late payments

Some severe **consequences** or "**painful side effects**" of Financial STDs are:

1. Lack of savings for emergencies
2. Reduction in credit score
3. Rise in loan interest rates
4. Phone calls and letters from Collection Agencies
5. Legal collection efforts, such as default judgments, garnishments, levies or liens

SOMETHING TO THINK ABOUT: Many people who are financially promiscuous and contract Financial STDs may begin the process of curing their financial dis-ease, but may stop the process of "financial medication" once the pain of the "common symptoms" stop. So they not only go out and continue their financially destructive behavior of financial promiscuity (spending money they do not have using revolving credit), they may also add a co-borrower or cosigner who may be unsuspecting or unknowing of their dormant financial dis-ease. This could result in that co-borrower or cosigner being susceptible to contracting the financial dis-ease and feeling the pain of the "common symptoms."

You never know who has a Financial Dis-Ease, like Financial STDs. Therefore, it is important for you to be extremely careful with whom you decide to share joint obligation of any debt with. Some people don't even know they have Financial STDs until it is too late.

It is important for every consumer to get a **FINANCIAL CHECK UP** at least once a year to avoid or deal with potential or existing Financial Dis-Eases. A Financial Check Up consists of:

1. **Writing out or updating a Budget or Spending Plan** to make sure all financial obligations are being taking care of, including savings. Make sure to list all monthly net income (take home pay) and expenses. Your income (take home pay) should be capable of being allocated for each type of expense.

   For example, here is a simple allocation to use:

   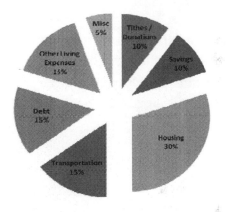

   a. **Tithe / Donations   -   10%**
   Tithe is the amount that goes to a church or charitable organization (and is a great tax write off might I add, or a moral obligation for many). If tithing is not executed, this percentage should be added to other areas such as savings, debt or other living expenses.

b. Savings - 10%

Savings is not play money. This is savings for unanticipated emergencies or planned wealth activities, like retirement. Make this a required bill that must be paid, on time and every time. Place the savings account somewhere so that it is not easily accessible. Consider an Investment Retirement Account (IRA) or Certificate of Deposit (CD) at your local credit union.

c. Housing - 30%

Housing expenses includes mortgage/rent, and any costs tied to it such as property taxes, utilities, water / sewer / garbage, cable / satellite, telephone, alarm systems, association fees, etc.

d. Transportation - 15%

Transportation expenses include car payment(s), gas, maintenance / repairs, insurance, tags, vehicle registration, tolls / parking / other means of transportation (bus), etc.

e. Debt - 15%

Debt expenses include unsecured loans, credit cards, student loans, and other loans from finance companies / payday lenders / furniture companies, etc.

f. Other Living Expenses - 15%

Other Living expenses include groceries, household items, lunches for at work / school, prescriptions / doctors' visits, daycare / sitter, child support, beauty / barber, dining out, sports / hobbies / clubs / gyms, cell phone, banking fees, etc.

g. Miscellaneous - 5%
Miscellaneous expenses include play money to go out with family / friends for dinner or going shopping for a new laptop or that new iPad. Reward yourself for working hard and paying all of your bills on time. This should only be allotted for and only spent once all of the expenses stated above have been satisfied.

 SOMETHING TO THINK ABOUT: If the housing expense takes up more than 30% or transportation takes up more than 15% of your net income (take home pay) and other bills still need to be paid as well, you may run the risk of financial dis-ease and want to consider altering some of your miscellaneous spending, downsizing or increasing your income.

There are several variations of this financial allocation. If you have more bills to pay out than you have income coming in; you have a Financial Dis-Ease, which could possibly be a Financial STD. We'll discuss possible cures in a few moments.

2. **Reviewing your credit report** to make sure the information is accurate and disputing any inaccurate information. There are several websites that can be used to pull all three major credit reports, but most 3 in 1 credit report websites are sponsored by one of the three major credit reporting companies. They are:

a. Equifax (www.equifax.com)

b. Experian (www.experian.com)

c. Trans Union (www.transunion.com)

We'll talk about them more when we talk about the Credit Game.

View your credit report as often as quarterly and at least once a year. By law you are entitled to at least one free credit report annually. In some states you may be entitled to more than one annually. You may request your credit report and credit score by visiting www.annualcreditreport.com

3. **Checking your credit score** to see if it has increased or decreased and find out why. You can purchase and view your credit score through the credit reporting company sites stated above or through www.freecreditscore.com.

   a. If your credit score has increased, consider requesting your financial institution to lower the interest rate on your revolving debt or refinance your installment debt at a lower interest rate. They may say no, however you won't know if you don't ask.

   b. If your credit score has decreased, you will certainly want to know why. If you are not familiar with reading your credit report to determine this, ask for help from a Credit Coach, or at your friendly local credit union (yes, that was a plug!). Other financial institutions may be willing to assist you as well.

Keep in mind that the Consumer Score that you purchase may be different by several points than the credit reports retrieved by financial institutions and other organizations and businesses. This is because there are numerous types of scoring models that credit reporting companies sell. For example, there are Consumer Purchased Scores, Lender / Financial Institution Scores, Auto Dealership Scores, Utility Scores (for utilities companies), etc.

So, what's the cure for Financial STDs?

Depending on how severe the financial disease is will determine how long or financially painful the process may be. It may require a minor financial procedure of altering your spending plan / budget or borrowing behaviors or it may require major surgery or financial abortion, like bankruptcy. (Yes, I said it.) Although I am not an advocate of bankruptcy, it may be necessary for certain financial situations.

Every cure for financial diseases has its own side effects that may cause temporary discomfort or may significantly and temporarily impact your financial health negatively. But, it may ultimately cure your financial disease. The thing to remember is that in order for the cure or the process to work, you will have to be ready and willing to change or alter your spending habits and borrowing behavior. If you fail to do this, the financial disease, like Financial STDs, will return with a vengeance!

Some helpful tips to beginning the process of curing Financial Dis-Eases are:

1. **STOP BORROWING!** (Financial Abstinence) Cease and desist using your available unsecured/revolving credit. Delay getting a loan for that new or used car unless it is absolutely necessary or if it will be less costly than maintaining your existing vehicle.

2. **HOW MUCH DO YOU OWE ANYWAY?** List all of your actual balances of all of your loans from all of your financial institutions or creditors. Make sure you write down your monthly payments and the interest rates you are paying for each debt.

3. **WALK UP THE MOUNTAIN, DON'T RUN!** Start with your smallest debt and try to pay that off first. Once that debt is paid off, use that money for payments toward the next debt … Keep that pace until all of your debts are paid in full.

For those of you that are saying under your breath, "Yeah right, if I could do that I wouldn't have to choose between paying my credit card bill, buying food for my family or paying for my utilities / rent / mortgage, etc." Duly noted. In this case, go get a FINANCIAL CHECK UP with a Financial Professional!!! This may not include your family, coworkers, best friend, etc. unless they are a Financial Professional.

Then again, you may not want them knowing all of your business like that anyway.

The Financial Professional or Credit Coach should be able to take all of your financial information and create a Budget/Spending Plan with Savings incorporated or provide you with HONEST feedback regarding your actual financial situation. If they are not HONEST with you and try to medicate your symptoms of financial disease with more loans, RUN don't walk ... RUN! You would not TOLERATE a medical doctor not being honest about your physical health, so don't TOLERATE a Financial Professional not being honest about your financial health. If the prognosis is bad, so be it. At least they should be able to share with you options and refer you to a financial specialist if they cannot assist you. That financial specialist just might be a bankruptcy attorney, but that should be your LAST resort, in my opinion.

Below are a few recommended financial prescriptions towards curing financial diseases.

Recommended Cures for Financial STDs

Symptoms	Financial Rx	Recommended Action
• Frequently Overdrawn Checking Account • No more than 30 days late on loan payments • No money for savings	*Financial Medication*	Modify Spending Habits by developing a Budget or Spending Plan

Recommended Cures for Financial STDs

Symptoms	Financial Rx	Recommended Action
• Several Overdrawn Checking Accounts • Using Credit Cards to pay household bills • Maxed out or maxing out credit cards • Always between 30 – 60 days late on loan payments • No money for savings	*Financial Abstinence with Financial Medication*	• Stop using revolving credit. • Reduce or stop unnecessary miscellaneous spending. • Develop a Spending Plan. • Contact financial institutions for payment plans on delinquent accounts / debts.
• Delinquent Overdrawn Checking Accounts • Maxed out credit cards • More than 60 days late on loan payments • Accounts in collections or reported as charged off • Facing foreclosure • Facing Repossession • Owe more in monthly debt than monthly take home pay	*Financial Surgery with Financial Medication & Financial Abstinence*	This should be done with a Financial Professional or through a financial education organization: • Stop using revolving credit. • Minimize miscellaneous spending. • Develop a budget. • Request a loan modification from creditors. • Request a payment modification. • Negotiate rate, term, or payment amount.

All previously stated recommended cures should be attempted and exhausted. If your financial condition is more severe and none of the previously stated recommendations work for curing your financial disease, you may then want to discuss your legal options. A financial legal option, which should be a last resort, is what I consider Financial Abortion, also known as bankruptcy, chapter 7: Liquidation (or Termination) of Debt.

Although I am not an advocate of bankruptcy, I am not opposed to it when there are no other alternatives or options available.

It is imperative that if you are considering this option, do your homework about this process and the possible financial consequences.

On a lighter note, in order to create or obtain a health Financial Relationship and avoid being Financially Promiscuous and possibly acquiring Financial STDs, I recommend that you Date Financial Institutions ... the RIGHT WAY!

5 WHAT IS FINANCIAL DATING?

Every consumer should DATE financial institutions. This does not mean you have to Commit to and have several Primary Financial Institutions (PFIs). This just means that you should shop around and get to know several different types of financial institutions in order to find that ONE that can give you 80% of what you NEED. We'll discuss the 80% Rule in the following chapter.

What is Financial Dating? Financial Dating consists of five phases: Exploration, Investigation, Introduction, Courting, and Commitment.

Exploration is when you are in the market for a new or additional financial institution (FI). You should begin looking and exploring your options. You may do this by asking friends, family members or coworkers; looking around your neighborhood; listening to commercials/media; or searching the World Wide Web.

Investigation is when you have found your option(s) and now wants to know a little bit more about the financial institution before you move further. So you may ask your family, friends, or colleagues about their experience with the financial institution(s). You may even go online to see if others have anything pertinent to say that may help you with your decision to move forward.

Introduction is when you have decided which financial institution(s) you are going to go to directly for more information. You should go to the financial institution and sit down with a Customer Service Representative to find out more about how to and some of the advantages of opening an account.

Courting is when you and the financial institution put on your best performance for one another. You have "lots of money" and "great credit." The financial institution has the "best rates" and "lots of services" that you need with "minimal to no fees."

Depending on how effective you are in your Investigation phase will determine if the financial institution is telling you the truth or if you will fall for what the financial institution tells you if they are not. In the same respect, depending on if the financial institution pulls your credit report during the account opening process may determine if they will cross sell you all of the products and services they were telling you about, or just open up a savings account for you and send you on your way. Regardless, this is your opportunity to really see how many of your "Deal Makers" and "Deal Breakers" the financial institution possess.

Commitment is when you have decided that the financial institution will be your Primary Financial Institution (PFI), which means that the financial institution will have your savings, checking and debit card, auto loan, home loan, first born child (ok not really). But they are taking care of the majority of your financial needs and you think of that financial institution first when you have a financial need or want.

Although Financial Dating has five phases, during your Financial Dating Spree, you should only proceed to the fifth phase when you have found a financial institution that satisfies 80% of your financial NEEDS.

Before you begin your Financial Dating Spree, there are a few things to consider to ensure that you are Financially Dating on PURPOSE and NOT haphazardly!

1. **What do you NEED?** NEEDS are "requirements." So, before you Financially Date, you should understand what your requirements are for a financial institution. Write out your "NEEDS" list so you can clearly understand your "deal makers." For example, "I need a checking account with a debit card to access my money."

2. **What do you WANT?** WANTS are "nice to haves." Again, before you Financially Date, you should understand what you WANT and what you do NOT want. Write down your "Wants/Don't Wants" list so that you clearly understand more of your "deal makers" and your "deal breakers." For example, "I WANT a financial institution with competitive loan rates." "I do NOT want a financial institution with extremely high fees."

3. **What are you willing to TOLERATE?** Not all
financial institutions are created equally for all
consumers. There are so many financial institutions
to choose from, so you have hundreds of options.
Therefore, there are certain things that you could or
should TOLERATE or NOT tolerate, because you
can. Write down your "Tolerate/Won't Tolerate" list
so that you will clearly understand what you may be
willing to compromise or more of your "deal
breakers." For example, "I can tolerate fewer
branches, which may mean I would have to drive
further." "I will NOT tolerate poor or rude customer
service."

Once you clearly understand these areas about your
NEEDS, WANTS, and what you will or will not
TOLERATE, you will be better prepared to Financially Date
on Purpose.

SOMETHING TO THINK ABOUT: Again ... "Not
all financial institutions are created equally or are for
everyone." It is important that you understand what
products and services the financial institutions, that you are
dating, are "good at" and not so "good at."

For example, let's look at Joe's personal situation. Joe is
a single man and decided that he wanted to get back on the
dating scene to find his future mate. Joe missed having a
home cooked meal every night and really wanted that again.
He dated a few women, but they did not like to cook or did
not cook often. So, one day he told one of them that he really
liked, "You need to cook for me more, like every night." She
ignored that requirement and he eventually ended the

relationship. Joe needed to determine if a woman's ability or desire to cook for him often was a "deal maker" or a "deal breaker."

If it was a "deal maker," it would have been nice if she cooked for him often (his WANT) but it is not required for him to pursue the relationship further. He may have been able to TOLERATE the fact that she did not cook for him often if she possessed other traits that benefited him as a help-mate or if she agreed to cook for him frequently instead of everyday.

Now, if this was a "deal breaker," then he should have terminated the conversation, interaction, and stopped dating her, like he did, because it was a NEED for him and was required for him to pursue the relationship further. In this scenario, he could NOT tolerate being with a woman that could not or would not cook for him.

This same scenario applies with dating a financial institution. If you require flexibility in their credit underwriting process because your credit may be a bit "colorful" and you go to a financial institution that is extremely conservative with their credit underwriting process, your expectation of an approval for the loan request may or may not happen. So don't get upset! If credit underwriting flexibility is a NEED, you may want to look for a financial institution (credit union) that already has this in place.

"How do I find this out?" you ask. Ask during the Investigation or Introduction phase. This will help you determine if Courting is really worth your time.

Financial Dating on Purpose helps you avoid dating numerous financial duds, which may waste your time and possibly money.

Take a few moments to think about and write down your "deal makers" and "deal breakers." This may NOT be easy, but it will be well worth it when it comes time for you to go on your Financial Date! Trust.

MY FINANCIAL DEAL MAKERS & DEAL BREAKERS

FINANCIAL NEED (DEAL MAKERS)
1.
2.
3.
4.
5.

FINANCIAL WANTS (DEAL MAKERS)	FINANCIAL DON'T WANTS (DEAL BREAKERS)
1.	1.
2.	2.
3.	3.
4.	4.
5.	5.

I CAN TOLERATE (COMPROMISE)	I WILL NOT TOLERATE (DEAL BREAKERS)
1.	1.
2.	2.
3.	3.
4.	4.
5.	5.

6 THE 80% RULE

Tyler Perry wrote it so well in the movie, "Why Did I Get Married." The gist was that in every good marriage / relationship your mate will give you at least 80% of what you NEED. You may be tempted by others that may have the 20% of what you WANT that you may not be getting from your spouse or significant other. That 20% may seem to be better or more attractive than the 80%, but in the end, the 20% will never be able to give you 80% of what you NEED.

A financial institution worthy of becoming your Primary Financial Institution (PFI) should be able to satisfy 80% of your financial NEEDS. Those financial institutions tempting you with the 20% of what you WANT may not ultimately be able to give you that 80% of what you NEED financially. If you fall for the 20% (WANT), you may realize that it really wasn't all you thought it was going to be.

For example: You get a postcard in the mail from a financial institution advertising auto loan rates as low as 2.99% and that you have been "Pre-Selected" to apply to finance or refinance your vehicle! This financial institution has several branches near your home and has the coolest commercials on TV. Although your Primary Financial

Institution is a local credit union about 10 miles away, this financial institution is right down the street, less than 2 miles, and the rate they are advertising is much lower than what you are paying now, which is about 9%. Even though your credit union provides you with wonderful personal service, they know your name and everything, as well as flexible credit underwriting; you decide you are going to go for it. Keep in mind that this will not be a Financial Date per se, because your plan is to go right into the Commitment Phase because you are so attracted to that 2.99% auto loan rate and the fact that they "Pre-Selected" YOU to apply.

You decide to go to the financial institution and apply for that 2.99% auto loan. While you're there, you decide to open up a savings and checking account. They even convinced you to switch your direct deposit from your credit union to them. WOW! You are excited about this new financial relationship.

About a week later you receive two letters from your New Primary Financial Institution. One is your new debit card for your checking account. Cool! The other is a letter regarding your auto loan refinance application request, which states that you were DENIED due to derogatory information reporting on your credit report. "HUH?" you think. "They Pre-Selected ME!"

You drive to your new Primary Financial Institution's branch down the street from your house to find out what's going on and see if they will reconsider their decision. The Customer Service Representative advises you that your loan application has been denied because of your "colorful credit" (You knew that already) and that there was nothing that they or you could do at this time. The decision was final. You just started your relationship with them (no history) and you are relatively new to the area and on your job.

PS. You figured out that your new checking account is NOT Free! So, you will be assessed monthly checking account and debit card service charges. Stop whining! They gave you the schedule of fees that you didn't bother to read when you opened the account. In your excitement, you've set up your HomeBanking and Bill Pay service with them, so you have your check coming into the account soon and bills coming out as soon as tomorrow from the deposit you made recently.

Now that 20% of what you wanted but didn't come through, doesn't seem as attractive as the 80% of what you needed that was being met by your friendly neighborhood credit union about 10 miles away.

This story is in no way meant to slant your perspective or opinion about other financial institutions. ☺ It is only a story to help you understand the importance of being aware of your NEEDS, WANTS, and what you will or will not TOLERATE.

Again, get to know the financial institution before you commit to a long-term financial relationship. Don't rush the relationship because of a financial temptation or because of a pre-mature financial break up with another financial institution. Make sure you take some time to step away and think about what you want out of the relationship and if the new financial institution can at least meet your 80% Rule.

 SOMETHING TO THINK ABOUT: When you are Financially Dating financial institutions, make sure they can satisfy 80% of your financial NEEDS before you jump into the Commitment Phase! This may possibly void a potential Financially Abusive relationship in the future.

7 ARE YOU BEING FINANCIALLY ABUSED?

A girl friend of mine was in an abusive relationship for many years. She wasn't happy but she was comfortable with her lifestyle with this man she was dating. Every time I visited her I was reminded why I vowed not to ever visit her home again. So every time I got amnesia and missed my friend, I would to go her house.

Anyway, she was <u>not</u> married to this man but living with him. He was attractive, had a great job and earned lots of money, very active in church, and well respected in the community. However, he verbally and emotionally abused my friend. He would talk down to her, call her names like stupid, idiot... (And those were the nice names). He, of course, hated me because I always had something to say to him to make him feel like... well, you know. "An eye for an eye!" I thought, so I would let him have it when he disrespected my friend in front of me. I was more upset with my friend because she allowed him to do it. "Are you serious?" I would say to her. "Why do you allow him to verbally abuse you like that?" "Mind your business." She would tell me. "I have a good life here and it would be too complicated to leave. We have everything together, this house, bank accounts, etc. As long as he doesn't hit me, it's whatever..." she would say nonchalantly. "HUH???" I would think, and then I would vow never to go back over to her house, again.

She was willing to be abused by a man (that she wasn't even married to) because it was too complicated to leave.

There were several mishaps with this relationship:

1. She was a co-borrower on a substantial purchase that she could not afford alone and with a man that she did not have a legally binding relationship with.

2. She comingled her money in a jointly owned bank account with a man that she did not have a legally binding relationship with. She gave him equal ownership of all of her money (direct deposit of her paycheck) and in the same respect she had equal ownership of his money (that he deposited) in that account. Later, she found out that he had other individual accounts that she wasn't aware of.

3. She sold her self-respect and self-esteem for what she thought was a financially stable lifestyle.

4. She taught him how to treat her early on by allowing him to disrespect and verbally abuse her.

As frustrating as it was for me to see her stay in this relationship; no matter what I told her and how much she knew I loved and wanted the best for her, she was not going to leave until she became sick and tired of her situation and was ready for a change.

Many of us are being Financially Abused by our financial institutions through poor service, high or frequent fees, ridiculously high loan interest rates, extremely low deposit rates, etc. You may have your home loan or car loan, direct deposit, some unsecured loans, credit cards, bill payment service, with this financial institution, but the financial institution continues to pass on more fees, won't lower interest rates, and have poor customer service. You may want to leave but may feel it would be too much trouble to change everything over to another financial institution that would probably treat you better.

The financial institution is not even giving you 80% of what you need. You may have skipped the beginning phases of Financial Dating and went straight into the Commitment Phase, and now you realize that the financial institution that tempted you with 20% of what you thought you financially wanted was not what you thought the financial institution would be.

You may have had some financial mishaps and have damaged credit, so who else is going to take you in and help improve your financial situation? You may feel that you may not be able to get what you need from other financial institutions because of your current financial or credit situation so it may just be better to deal with the Financial Abuse and keep everything the way it is. Right? WRONG!

If you are being Financially Abused, now is the time to plan your exit strategy. It is not wise to make irrational moves, so don't go into your financial institution and scream "I'M MAD AS HELL, AND I'M NOT TAKING IT

ꓶYMORE!!!" That would be like quitting your job before ou have found a new one.

Assess the Depth of Your Current Financial Relationship

Before you can begin creating an exit strategy, you must understand how deep you are in the financial relationship with your current financial institution. For example, are you just Financially Dating (have a checking or savings account) or are you in a Committed Financial Relationship and have unsecured (not secured by collateral), revolving credit (like credit cards or lines of credit), auto loan(s), mortgage loans, direct deposit, bill pay, etc.

The following exercise will help you determine the depth of your financial relationship. Remember, the deeper the Financial Relationship, the more of a challenge it may be to terminate or leave quickly without possible and potential financial hardships. It does not mean that you can't "exit stage left!" It just means that if you are not careful and move too hastily, you may end up with financial causalities on your credit report.

EXERCISE: Select every service you are using at the financial institution.

Deposit Accounts & Services

- ❏ Savings Account(s)
- ❏ Checking Account(s)
- ❏ Certificate of Deposits (CDs)
- ❏ IRA(s)
- ❏ Money Market Account(s)
- ❏ ATM/Debit Card(s)
- ❏ Direct Deposit

Loans

- ❏ Credit Card
- ❏ Unsecured Loan
- ❏ Auto Loan(s)
- ❏ Home Equity Loan / Second Mortgage
- ❏ 1st Mortgage Loan
- ❏ Student Loan(s)
- ❏ Secured Loan(s)

Online Services

- ❏ Online / Home Banking
- ❏ Bill Payment Service (List bills being paid through service)

Other Services or Accounts

- ❏ _____
- ❏ _____
- ❏ _____

What is this Financial Relationship Costing You?

Determine how much interest and fees you are paying to this financial institution for one month. Your monthly statement from the previous month should help you figure this out.

How much did you pay in fees?

- ❏ Non-Sufficient Funds (NSF) Fees $_____
- ❏ Courtesy Pay / Over Draft Fees $_____
- ❏ ATM / Debit Card Fees $_____
- ❏ Past Due Loan Fees $_____
- ❏ Other Loan Fees $_____

How much are you paying in interest on your loans?

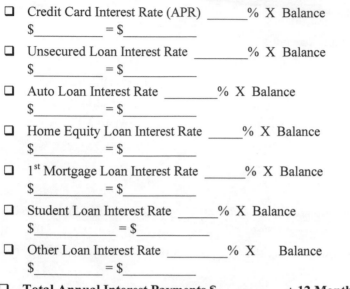

- ☐ Credit Card Interest Rate (APR) _____% X Balance
  $_____ = $_____

- ☐ Unsecured Loan Interest Rate _____% X Balance
  $_____ = $_____

- ☐ Auto Loan Interest Rate _____% X Balance
  $_____ = $_____

- ☐ Home Equity Loan Interest Rate _____% X Balance
  $_____ = $_____

- ☐ 1st Mortgage Loan Interest Rate _____% X Balance
  $_____ = $_____

- ☐ Student Loan Interest Rate _____% X Balance
  $_____ = $_____

- ☐ Other Loan Interest Rate _____% X Balance
  $_____ = $_____

- ☐ **Total Annual Interest Payments $_____ ÷ 12 Months =
  $_____ Monthly Interest Payment**

Now, add up your monthly Interest payments and monthly Fees to see what this financial relationship is costing you.

My Total Monthly Interest Payment $_____ + My Total Monthly Fees $_____ Equals My <u>Monthly Financial Relationship Costs</u> (MFRC) $_____.

If your Monthly Financial Relationship Costs are more than 30% - 40% of your monthly Net Income (Take Home Pay), you may be in a financially abusive relationship. Therefore, you may want to nip some spending behaviors in the bud now to minimize or stop the excessive fees; or consider working on your exit strategy.

If your Monthly Financial Relationship Costs are more than 50%, you are definitely in a financially abusive relationship and you need to start planning your exit strategy ASAP!

SOMETHING TO THINK ABOUT: In order to estimate how much in interest payments you are paying on your revolving loans annually, take your loan balance and multiply it by the interest rate or annual percentage rate (APR). For a quick monthly figure, divide the amount by 12. That's around about the amount you are paying in interest monthly.

Keep in mind that this amount will change as the balance decreases or increases. Most revolving loans have compounded interest which simply means that you will <u>pay interest on the interest that accrued the previous month plus the principle balance</u> if your monthly payment does not cover all of the prior month's interest.

Also, in case you didn't know, the order in which your payments may normally be applied to your loan is:
1) Accrued Interest (cost of the loan),
2) Fees (cost of possibly doing something wrong – late payment, over the limit, etc.), then, if anything is left over;
3) The Principal (what you borrowed).

The larger the balance, the more interest you will pay… and just know that the financial institution is going to get their profit (interest and fees) upfront!

For those of you who need a visual example… here goes. You have a $5,000 balance on your credit card. Multiply that

18.00% APR. This will give you an estimation of the annual interest you may pay (every year until the balance is reduced or paid in full) of $900.00. Divided this amount by 12 months. This will give you an estimation of the interest you may pay monthly of $75.00. So, if you only pay a minimum payment of 2.00% of the balance, which is $100.00, only $25.00 will be paid on the balance and the $75.00 will be paid to the monthly interest amount due. Oh... BUT WAIT!!! If there was a fee or fees assessed within that monthly statement period, like a $35.00 late payment fee; instead of the $25.00 paying on the balance, it will be applied to the fee charged. Which, in this example, $25.00 would be applied to the fee assessed and would leave a new balance of $10 which would be added to your $5,000 balance. Yeah! Now your new balance is $5,010.00.

This is a simplified example of how interest is calculated. The amount of interest owed is usually based on an Average Daily Balance which is your average balance during that month.

The following is an example of this simple calculation for a three month payment period. Look closely at how much is paid to interest and fees, as well as how much is paid or added to the balance when only the minimum payment is paid.

	Month 1	Month 2	Month 3
Current Revolving Balance	**$5,000.00**	**$5,010.00**	**$4,984.95**
(X) APR	18.00%	18.00%	18.00%
(=) Annual Interest Payment	$900.00	$901.80	$897.29
(÷) 12 Mos.	$75.00	$75.15	$74.77
(+) Fees	$35.00	$0.00	$0.00
(=) Total Mo. Int. + Fees	$110.00	$75.15	$74.77
Required Min. Payment (2%)	-$100.00	-$100.20	-$99.70
Amount Paid to Balance	**+$10.00**	**-$25.05**	**-$24.92**

Can you imagine how long it will take you to pay this balance in full?

Below reflects how much would be paid to the balance, interest, and fees in those three months:

Payment Category	**Total Payments**
Paid on Balance	**$15.05**
Paid to Interest	$224.92
Paid to Fee	$35.00

Do the math with your revolving credit balance. Always try to pay more than the minimum payment required to make sure that the balance will get paid after the interest and fees.

Now that we clarified that, let's discuss an Exit Strategy from a Financially Abusive Relationship.

Exit Strategy when you are Just "Financially Dating" the Financial Institution

If you only partake in a few products and services of the financial institution (FI) like a checking account with a debit card, savings account, home (internet) banking, etc., then you should:

1. **HOLD OUT!** Stop giving it up (financially). Stop overdrawing your account by carefully balancing your checkbook / account, as much as possible. If your account is negative, contact the financial institution to see if they would be willing to refund all or a few of the fees as a one-time courtesy, if possible, to reduce the amount you may have to pay back before you close the account.

2. **GET BACK OUT ON THE FINANCIAL DATING SCENE!** Begin the steps of Financially Dating pointed out in Chapter 5. Do NOT skip the Phases! Follow them in order and do NOT execute Phase 5: Commitment, until you are absolutely sure that the financial institution passes your 80% Rule! Trust me on this one.

3. **SHUT IT DOWN!** Once you have found a potentially new financial institution, begin to transition your money and service usage to the new financial institution. For example, withdraw the funds that are in your old financial institution's account and close it, then open a savings account with the new financial institution and deposit those funds into your new savings account. Consult with your new financial institution's customer service department to discuss and determine the best way to

make your other transitions from the old financial institution to the new one.

4. **MAKE THEM EARN IT!** What I have observed is that when most people get excited about any new relationship, the one who likes the other more, may give up "too much, too soon and too fast." Therefore, in your angst and excitement to build this new financial relationship and get out of your current financially abusive relationship, PLEASE PROCEED WITH CAUTION and move at a moderate pace to build a deeper financial relationship with the new financial institution. Make them earn your business!

Exit Strategy when you are "Financially Married" to the Financial Institution

You may be financially married to a financial institution if they have financed your mortgage, seconded mortgage, home equity loan, line of credit, auto loan, credit card(s), student loans, etc. You get the picture. They are your Primary Financial Institution (PFI). The financial relationship started off great!!! Somewhere after you lost your job, got furloughed, or became financially promiscuous, the relationship began to deteriorate. It may not even have been your fault. The financial institution may have made changes due to the economic environment to protect itself, or because of the unexpected and possibly unrealistic modifications required by federal regulations. Regardless of who moved … it's just not the same and is possibly becoming financially abusive.

Reality Check: If you have good credit and a high credit score, the Exit Strategy may be as easy and as fast as you getting approved for a loan at another financial institution to pay off the loan at your primary financial institution at a lower interest rate.

If you have "colorful" or damaged credit and a low credit score, the Exit Strategy may be a challenge and may take more time for you to find a viable financial institution that may be understanding and flexible to your situation of past financial indiscretions.

Because your financial relationship is so deep and significant, you may want to consider trying to work it out by meeting with a Customer Service Representative, Branch Manager, Loan Manager, or Collection Manager, so that you and your primary financial institution can come to a compromise. That compromise may be to change the type of account you have so you won't have to pay so many monthly service changes on your checking account. It may be a modification to your home or auto loan payment. Whatever it is, attempt to work it out before you do anything irrational. At the end of the day, it may be you and your credit that will ultimately get hurt.

As with any break up, you should talk with a professional. Call me…

8 FINANCIAL ABSTINENCE

At some point enough is enough! After dealing with the pain and consequences of Financial STDs and other Financial Dis-Eases because of Financial Promiscuity; after all of the creditors that you had long term financial relationships with, that should have been Financial One Night Stands; and after suffering Financial Abuse for so long, it's time to just STOP! There will come a time when doing things the way you have always done them (financially) will NOT yield you different or better results. Therefore, time must be taken to assess your current financial situation and remove yourself from financial temptations and distractions.

Financial Abstinence may take up to 30 days, months or several years depending on how financially damaged you are. Financial Abstinence is refraining from any indulgence of using revolving and other available credit. This will help you establish a baseline of your current financial and credit situation and determine how much you owe and how much debt must be repaid. Once you have established where you are financially, you can then decide where you want to be financially and determine what amount of time you need by

tablishing your Short-Term, Medium-Term, and Long-
rm financial goals. Don't worry … it's not that difficult.
Think of it this way: You want to take a vacation to
alifornia and you live in New York. Because of whatever
limitations, you have determined that it will be best to drive.
Your GPS is not working so you have to rely on a map. In
order for you to determine how to get to your final
destination, you must:

1. Identify your exact location. Where exactly are you
   (beginning destination)?

2. Identify your final destination. Where exactly do you
   want to go (final destination)?

3. Identify your needs to get there. Are you going to rent a
   car or drive your own car? How much gas will be
   needed? What does gas cost now, anyway? How many
   times will you have to stop to fill up? How much
   spending money will you need for miscellaneous
   expenses like lodging (if necessary) or eating? Who's
   going with you and will they chip in or be an added
   expense? Whew!

4. Identify your Short-Term Goal. Where will your first
   stop be to fill up for gas and eat?

5. Identify your Medium-Term Goal. Where are you going
   to stop to rest (possible lodging)? Will you need to fill up
   again or eat?

6. Identify your Long-Term Goal. Where are you going t
stay when you arrive at your final destination? How lon,
are you planning to stay? How much money will you
need? Are you returning to your starting destination or
will you be staying at your final destination permanently?
Etc. etc. etc.

This same concept should be applied to your financial
situation. The purpose of Financial Abstinence is to help you
to execute step #1: Identify your exact location (financially).
How much do you really owe?

SOMETHING TO THINK ABOUT: If you keep
moving around, you will not be able to determine
your exact location and therefore you may not be able
to accurately determine the most effective route to take to
your final destination. Likewise, if you keep using credit,
you will not be able to determine exactly how much you owe
and therefore, you may not be able to determine what will be
necessary (for monthly payments or to pay off the debt) to
reach your short, medium, and long term financial goals.

Financial Abstinence is not easy! But it becomes
financially liberating when you begin to see your credit debt
decrease, your Financial STDs and Financial Dis-Eases being
cured, your Financial Reputation (on your credit reports)
improving, and you realize that you no longer have to stay in
or deal with Financially Abusive Relationships. You become
emotionally empowered when you regain your power over
your financial situation.

Financial Abstinence does not mean to close down your
revolving accounts. If you do that, it may negatively affect

ur credit score. It just means to not use the available
redit! So cut up the plastic, but leave the account(s) open.

It is always good to enlist the support of someone who is
knowledgeable about financial and credit matters, like a
Financial Professional or Credit Coach, to guide you through
this process of planning and to help encourage you when you
feel that financial temptation, like that One Day Sale at
Macy's. I digress...

CAUTION!!! Be very careful when deciding to get back
out onto that Financial Dating Scene. If you are not careful,
you may be tempted by the wrong Financial Partner and find
yourself in the same or worse financial situation than before.
So don't rush! When the time, Financial Partner, and
purchase are right or necessary, you will find that it will not
negatively impact your financial situation and goals.

Also, you will notice that when you stop using revolving
credit and begin paying your debt down, creditors will try to
entice you to get more credit at a "low rate." Remain
steadfast in your Financial Abstinence until the time,
Financial Partner, and purchase is right!

So ... play hard to get!

9 THE CREDIT GAME: BOOK SNEAK PREVIEW

You've been through so much financially. Whether it was due to lack of knowledge, lack of control, lack of financial resources, lack of employment, or because of someone else's "lack," you are now faced with the task of cleaning up a past financial mess. Although your credit reputation may have improved because you are now paying your bills on time, there may be past credit issues that keep creeping up or that are still negatively impacting your credit score.

If this is the case, you must now realize that credit is a Game with players, positions, and rules. You are playing and are a player in the Credit Game by default because you have established and are using credit. If you do not know the players, their positions, and the rules, you will find yourself losing this expensive game.

Now, let's discuss this Credit Game, the players, their positions, the rules and then possible ways for you to "rebound" and ultimately win!

Point of Clarification

First, let's get some clarity. Although the three major credit reporting companies are referred to as Credit "Bureaus" or Credit "Agencies," they are **NOT** owned or operated by the government. The three major Credit Reporting Companies: Equifax, Experian, and Trans Union, along with their good friend Fair Isaac Corporation (*FICO*), are privately owned businesses.

Secondly, there are laws that govern credit reporting and collection activities. The Fair Debt Collection Protection Act (FDCPA) governs the institutions, legal entities or persons that execute collection activities and also protects the consumer. The Fair Credit Reporting Act (FRCA) governs the creditors, businesses, organizations or persons that report information to the credit reporting companies. It is the responsibility of the creditors, reporting institutions or persons, to report "accurate" information. The credit reporting companies report what they are given and search for public record information in order to add to the consumers' credit reports to make it more appealing for organizations to want to purchase credit reports and credit scores from them.

Yes, these privately owned businesses make money off of the creditors, institutions and persons that want to report **to them**, as well as profit from the institutions or persons that want to view consumer credit reports and obtain credit scores **from them**.

Credit Game Players

Every game has Players. The players of the Credit Game are

- The **Credit Reporting Companies:** Equifax, Experian, and Trans Union. They are all in cahoots with their good buddy FICO, also known as the "Credit Score."

- The **Reporting Creditor, Institution, or Person**. They are going to tell all of your financial business! Especially when you mess up and miss a payment.

- The **Consumer**. That's You!

Credit Game Player Positions & Strategy

Each Player has its own Position and Strategy to WIN the Credit Game!!!

- The **Credit Reporting Companies**: Their position and strategy is to report the information they receive from all who pay to report to them or that they have found through Public Record (Bankruptcy, Liens, Judgments, etc.). They want to MAKE as much MONEY as possible by getting creditors and other organizations / institutions to pay to report to them and by getting creditors and other businesses (employers, insurance companies, cell phone providers, utilities, etc.) to pay them to view consumers' Credit Reputation … I mean Credit Reports and Credit Scores.

The **Creditors, Institutions, or Persons**: Their position and strategy is to report financial information "accurately" as well as use the credit report to justify their financial decision and interest rate assignment. They want to MAKE as much MONEY off of the consumers as possible. The LOWER the Credit Score, the presumed HIGHER Risk; therefore, the HIGHER the loan interest rates, fees, cost of service, etc. will be. This is commonly known as "Risk Based Pricing." Keep in mind that some financial institutions want to protect their membership or customer base from excessive fees and high interest rates, like some bank and the Credit Union Movement. But... at the end of the day, all Financial Institutions, like all other businesses, are in it to make money.

- The **Consumer**. Your position and strategy is to purchase money to pay for goods or obtain services at a reasonable or lower cost. You want to SAVE as much MONEY as you can when you obtain a loan to purchase goods and pay less for services.

The Rules of the Credit Game

Every game has rules and here are the two significant rules of the Credit Game.

Rule #1: Understand that whatever you do financially and how you pay it back will be reported on your Credit Report and will affect your Credit Score. So don't mess up!!!

Ok, so if you've messed up with Rule #1... Rule #2 of the **Credit Game** has two parts: Consumer Behavior and

Consumer Knowledge. The Consumer Behavior part of Rule #2 involves:

1. Becoming Financially Abstinent and determining how much you owe and how much you can afford to pay.

2. Contacting your creditors to make payment arrangements, if necessary and if possible.

3. Contacting a Financial Professional to help you diagnose your Financial Dis-Ease and prescribe the most appropriate financial medication or necessary financial plan of action. Remember, it may be as simple as spending habit modification or as major as bankruptcy. Caution: Bankruptcy has consequences and may not always be the right cure, therefore should be considered as the last resort.

The Consumer Knowledge part of Rule #2 requires you to know and understand the following federal regulations: Fair Credit Reporting Act (FCRA) and the Fair Debt Collection Protection Act (FDCPA). If you are unaware or do not understand your rights and protection under these federally regulated laws, you may find yourself consistently losing the Credit Game and making the wrong decisions as it relates to the Consumer Behavior part of Rule #2. This may ultimately be detrimental to your financial situation.

If you do not know what you need to know in the Consumer Knowledge part of this rule, your credit score may probably be low and you are more than likely paying very high loan interest and fees, in essence, losing the Credit

Game. However, if you understand this part of the rule or partner with a Financial Professional or Organization who will educate you on your rights and protection within these federally regulated laws, you can rebound, and ultimately win this Credit Game!

So who will teach you the Consumer Knowledge part of this Rule of the Credit Game? You can educate yourself on financial and credit management or seek organizations or financial advisors to assist in your credit education.

SOMETHING TO THINK ABOUT: Most consumers expect Financial Institutions to teach them the rules of the game. Please understand that your opponent may not always be willing to share with you everything you need to know on how to win the game that they too are playing and trying to win. The unfortunate reality is, the less you know, the more you will ultimately pay the creditor or financial institution or service provider.

FCRA and FDCPA are ACTs and are substantial in size with significant amount of information, which may require possible legal interpretation in order for you to understand and use these laws to your benefit. BUT... it is so important for you to know and understand these laws. Every consumer has access to these Federally Regulated ACTs. These ACTs can be accessed by going to the following websites:

- Fair Credit Reporting Act (FCRA)
  http://www.ftc.gov/os/statutes/fcradoc.pdf

- Fair Debt Collection Protection Act (FDCPA)
  http://www.ftc.gov/bcp/edu/pubs/consumer/credit/cre27.pdf

A Winning Strategy

You should exercise your rights and protection under the Fair Credit Reporting Act, since more than 70% of the information on the credit report may be inaccurate or outdated; and the Fair Debt Collection Protection Act, in the event there are collection agencies that use unscrupulous and unlawful means and tactics to collect a debt that they purchased from or are collecting on behalf of another creditor. Should you not be able to interpret or understand these two significant federal regulations, it may be appropriate to contact a Financial Professional, like myself, or Consumer Advocate Legal Counsel, or a nonprofit organization that can educate you on your rights and protection, as well as assist you with possibly restoring your credit.

You will find that winning the Credit Game consists of 90% Financial and Credit Education. Ten percent may be through Consumer Behavior modification and Credit Restoration through the law. Credit Restoration is not the same as Credit Repair. Be very careful of Credit Repair Chop Shops and do your homework!!!

The Financial Rebound

By winning the Credit Game, you will be able to use your Credit and Credit Score as leverage and negotiation power to refinance your debt at a lower interest rate, paying less in fees and for services, get hired for that job, purchase that home or needed car, etc.

Then … experience the joy and benefits of bouncing back and enjoy the Credit Game! WINNING!

10 THE CONCLUSION: THE TALK

During a lively discussion I had via Facebook, it was discussed how traditionally there came a time when parents would sit their children down and have "The Talk" about sex or "the birds and the bees." It was revealed that many of their parents did not actually give them "The Talk," for whatever reason. Well ... this explains a great deal about why we have relationships and sexuality issues of society. That's another topic for another book.

The question that came to mind during this virtual conversation is "Are parents having 'The Talk' about credit and finances with their children like they are or should be having about sex?" The sad reality and response to this question was "NO!" The, somewhat, explanation to this sad reality of an answer is that a parent or adult cannot successfully teach a child a subject that they have not been taught, learned, or mastered themselves.

So, which comes first? The chicken or the egg? Who should get "The Talk" first? The parents, so that they will change their financial behaviors and teach their children? Or, the children, so they can show and teach their parents, avoid ossible financial and credit pitfalls, and then when they become parents, they can give their children "The Financial and Credit Talk."

Regardless of who gets it first, someone has to begin this crucial conversation to expose the truths, dismiss the fallacies, educate financial and credit strategies, and build credit leverage.

The purpose of having "The Talk" about finances and credit is to share the truth, reality and beauty of what credit should be, when credit "should be used," and what to expect from a future financial partner to avoid getting into a financially abusive relationship. Also, to share the virtue of credit while the child is young from someone who loves and cares for them.

Below are a few suggestions that may help guide you as you have "The Talk" about credit with your children, parents, siblings, family, friends, or coworkers. Everyone needs "The Talk!"

"The Talk" Suggestions:

1. Credit is meant to be used as leverage not to be a hindrance.

   a. Good Credit = High Credit Score = Credit Approval, Lower Interest Rates, Less Expensive Services, Job Opportunities, etc.

   b. Bad Credit = Low Credit Score = Credit Denials, Higher Interest Rates, More Expensive Services, Job Opportunity Rejection, etc.

2. Live within your means. Do not live a GROSS lifestyle on NET income.

   The amount of most loans approved by a creditor is based on your Gross Income. However, you only have the Net Income (after income taxes and deductions) as take home pay to pay all of your bills.

   For example, 35% for housing of a gross monthly income of $3,000 is $1,050, which is actually 44% of your net monthly income of $2,400 (after taxes and deductions). This means that monthly expenses may exceed your monthly take home pay.

   If this is the case, you will need to reduce your expenses or increase your income.

3. Involve your child(ren) with paying monthly bills or at least understanding the expenses involved with running a household, credit obligations, and savings.

4. Plan, Save, Buy.

   With smaller purchases, it is best to plan for the purchase, give yourself time to save for the expense and pay for the purchase in cash.

   Suggestion: Open an account for your child. Manage it and watch it grow together. Let them set their own financial goals to save up for to buy what they want on their own.

5. Become your own creditor.
Once you have established savings and you need to borrow money, LEND yourself the money with an interest Rate.

For example: You've saved $1.500. You need to borrow $1,000 from your savings. Charge yourself 18% APR. Multiply $1,000 by 1.18 to get the total amount you will need to pay yourself back, which will be $1,180.

Determine when you will want to replenish the savings account with the amount borrowed. This will be the term. Divide the number of monthly, weekly, bi-weekly payments by the total amount that will be due.

For example, $1,180 divided by 12 months equals $98.33/monthly payments you will owe to your savings.

6. Understand the Anatomy of the Credit Score:

35% Payment History, 30% Balances versus Credit Limits, 15% Types of Credit, 10% Length of Credit History, 10% Who's Looking at Your Credit.

Paying on time and revolving balances compared to the credit limit available equals 65% of the Credit Score.

So, pay your bills on time and don't be Financially Promiscuous! Keep your revolving balances less than 50% of the credit limits (preferably 10% or less).

7. Balance your bank account monthly. Pay close attention to how much and the types of fees you are paying.

   Fees can become a dangerous, ever changing and increasing bill if it is not monitored and controlled early.

   If you are not good at or don't know how to balance a checkbook or account, try splitting your paycheck up into 2 to 3 different accounts. One account for savings, another account for all of your bills you have to pay monthly, biweekly, weekly, or semi-monthly, and another account for your play money. This way you won't use your bill money "inadvertently" when you want to use your play money.

   Suggestion: Instead of opening more than 2 accounts, consider putting your "Play" money on a reloadable pre-paid card with a credit card logo, like MasterCard. This will help with modifying and controlling your spending habits as well as help you pay your bills timely.

This is a good start.

"The Talk" regardless if it is about sex, relationships, finances or credit, timing and maturity is important. But the conversation about money should begin when the child gets their first dollar!

I hope this book has encouraged you to want to continue this conversation towards a more healthy and prosperous financial well-being. I look forward to helping you through your new financial journey.

Best wishes!

THE BEGINNING...

APPENDIX: BLANK WORKSHEETS

AM I FINANCIALLY PROMISCUOUS?

❏ YES   ❏ NO   Are you using more and more of your income to pay towards your debt?

❏ YES   ❏ NO   Are you only making the minimum payments on your revolving credit cards or lines of credit?

❏ YES   ❏ NO   Are you using your credit card to pay bills or things that should be paid with cash?

❏ YES   ❏ NO   Are you paying bills with money that should be used to pay another bill or that should be saved to pay something else of importance? ("Robbing Peter to pay Paul?")

❏ YES   ❏ NO   If your credit card is declined when used, do you pull out another credit card (praying that the transaction will go through) because you did not have enough cash or money in your bank account to cover the purchase?

❏ YES   ❏ NO   Are you frequently or sometimes late with your payments on credit obligations?

❏ YES   ❏ NO   Have you maxed out your credit cards or are you near the credit limit(s)?

❏ YES   ❏ NO   If you were approved for a loan or credit card at one financial institution, would you or have you gone to another financial institution to apply for more credit?

If you answered YES to any one of the questions, you may be considered Financial Promiscuous and susceptible to Financial STDs.

DO I HAVE FINANCIAL STDS?

Unsecured / Revolving Debt: List all unsecured / revolving debts including the name of the creditor, interest rate, monthly minimum payment, and total balance due. *Unsecured / revolving loans include unsecured installment loans, personal loans, credit cards, charge cards, etc.*

Creditor Name	Interest Rate	Monthly Payment	Balance
1.			
2.			
3.			
4.			
5.			
6.			
7.			
Total			

Secured Debt: List all secured debts including the name of the creditor, interest rate, monthly minimum payment, and total balance due. *Secured loans include real estate loans, auto/vehicle installment loans, savings secured loans, etc.*

Creditor Name	Interest Rate	Monthly Payment	Balance
1.			
2.			
3.			
4.			
5.			
6.			
7.			
Total			

Total Net Income / Take Home Pay	

BUILDING MY BUDGET / SPENDING PLAN

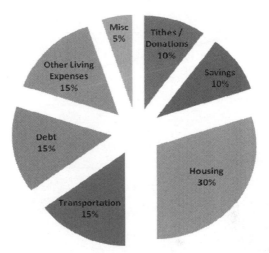

Category	%age	Times (X)	Monthly Net Pay	Equals	Budget Amount
Housing	30%	X	$	=	$
Transportation	15%	X	$	=	$
Debt	15%	X	$	=	$
Other Living Exps	15%	X	$	=	$
Tithes/Donations	10%	X	$	=	$
Savings	10%	X	$	=	$
Miscellaneous	5%	X	$	=	$

This is an example of monthly Net / Take Home Pay allocations that can get you started. There are numerous variations as to how to allocate your monthly Take Home Pay. Use monthly income allocations that are best for your financial situation.

MY FINANCIAL DEAL MAKERS & DEAL BREAKERS

FINANCIAL NEED (DEAL MAKERS)
1.
2.
3.
4.
5.

FINANCIAL WANTS (DEAL MAKERS)	FINANCIAL DON'T WANTS (DEAL BREAKERS)
1.	1.
2.	2.
3.	3.
4.	4.
5.	5.

I CAN TOLERATE (COMPROMISE)	I WILL NOT TOLERATE (DEAL BREAKERS)
1.	1.
2.	2.
3.	3.
4.	4.
5.	5.

Before getting out in the Financial Dating scene, it is important for your to know and understand your financial needs, wants, don't wants, what you will compromise, and what you will not tolerate. Then, follow the 5 phases of Financially Dating to find that Financial Institution that meets the 80% Rule.

HOW DEEP IS MY FINANCIAL RELATIONSHIP?

EXERCISE: Select every service you are using at the financial institution.

Deposit Accounts & Services

- ❑ Savings Account(s)
- ❑ Checking Account(s)
- ❑ Certificate of Deposits (CDs)
- ❑ IRA(s)
- ❑ Money Market Account(s)
- ❑ ATM/Debit Card(s)
- ❑ Direct Deposit

Loans

- ❑ Credit Card
- ❑ Unsecured Loan
- ❑ Auto Loan(s)
- ❑ Home Equity Loan / Second Mortgage
- ❑ 1st Mortgage Loan
- ❑ Student Loan(s)
- ❑ Secured Loan(s)

Online Services

- ❑ Online / Home Banking
- ❑ Bill Payment Service (List bills being paid through service)

Other Services or Accounts

- ❑ _____
- ❑ _____
- ❑ _____

How much is this Financial Relationship Costing You?

Determine how much interest and fees you are paying to this financial institution for one month. Your monthly statement from the previous month should help you figure this out.

How much did you pay in fees?

- ❑ Non-Sufficient Funds (NSF) Fees $_____
- ❑ Courtesy Pay / Over Draft Fees $_____
- ❑ ATM / Debit Card Fees $_____
- ❑ Past Due Loan Fees $_____
- ❑ Other Loan Fees $_____

How much are you paying in interest on your loans?

- ❑ Credit Card Interest Rate (APR) _____% X Balance $_____ = $_____
- ❑ Unsecured Loan Interest Rate _____% X Balance $_____ = $_____
- ❑ Auto Loan Interest Rate _____% X Balance $_____ = $_____
- ❑ Home Equity Loan Interest Rate _____% X Balance $_____ = $_____
- ❑ 1st Mortgage Loan Interest Rate _____% X Balance $_____ = $_____
- ❑ Student Loan Interest Rate _____% X Balance $_____ = $_____
- ❑ Other Loan Interest Rate _____% X Balance $_____ = $_____
- ❑ **Total Annual Interest Payments $_____ ÷ 12 Months = $_____ Monthly Interest Payment**

Add up your monthly Interest payments and monthly Fees to see what this financial relationship is costing you.

My Total Monthly Interest Payment $_____ + My Total Monthly Fees $_____ Equals My Monthly Financial Relationship Costs (MFRC) $_____.

Note: If your Monthly Financial Relationship Costs are more than 30% - 40% of your monthly Net Income (Take Home Pay), you may be in a financially abusive relationship. Therefore, you may want to nip some spending behaviors in the bud now to minimize or stop the excessive fees; or consider working on your exit strategy. If your Monthly Financial Relationship Costs are more than 50%, you are definitely in a financially abusive relationship and you need to start planning your exit strategy ASAP!

RESOURCES

CREDIT REPORTING COMPANIES

Equifax	Experian	Transunion
P.O. Box 740241	P.O. Box 9532	2 Baldwin Place
Atlanta, GA 30374	Allen, TX 75013	P.O. Box 1000
(800) 685-1111	(888) 397-3742	Chester, PA 19022
www.equifax.com	www.experian.com	(800) 888-4213
		www.transunion.com

ANNUAL CREDIT REPORT
www.annualcreditreport.com

CONSUMERS ACCESS TO FREE CREDIT REPORTS
www.ftc.gov/bcp/edu/pubs/consumer/credit/cre34.shtm

FAIR CREDIT REPORTING ACT (FCRA)
www.ftc.gov/os/statutes/fcradoc.pdf

FAIR DEBT COLLECTION PROTECTION ACT (FDCPA)
www.ftc.gov/bcp/edu/pubs/consumer/credit/cre27.pdf

FINANCIAL LIFE CONNECTION
www.financiallifeconnection.com

LOVE MY CREDIT UNION
www.lovemycreditunion.org

MYFICO CREDIT EDUCATION
www.myfico.com/crediteducation

OPERATION HOPE (BANKING ON OUR FUTURE)
www.operationhope.org

ABOUT THE AUTHOR

Tarra Jackson, a native of Dover, Delaware, is a single parent who has experienced financial and credit adversities. Tarra is an executive of a credit union in Atlanta, Georgia, as well as a credit coach and advisor to many entertainers. A graduate of Strayer University in Alexandria, VA, Tarra has over 15 years of experience within the financial services industry. Tarra is an energetic and charismatic public speaker who has spoken at numerous conferences and training events nationally and internationally.

Tarra prides herself in being a Financial Practitioner to help diagnose financial diseases and assist in prescribing financial and behavioral solutions through credit education and credit restoration. She is well respected in the industry for her honest, no-nonsense, tough love approach with credit coaching and counseling.

Tarra offers Credit Educational Seminars and Financial Boot Camps to promote Financial Well-Being through Credit Education! To book Tarra Jackson for a Credit Educational Seminar or a Financial Boot Camp, contact ProsperityNow.Bookings@gmail.com.

Made in the USA
Charleston, SC
10 July 2011